nimroz

PROVINCIAL HANDBOOK / A Guide to the People and the Province

Map of Nimroz

——	Road
⋯⋯	Dirt Track
▨▨▨	District Border
——	River
⊙	Provincial Capital
●	City

LOWER ELEVATION   HIGHER ELEVATION

Farah

Khash Rod

Delaram

Delaram

1

9

Lokhi

Khash Rod

Kang

Kang

Chakhansur

Zaranj

Chakhansur

Chakhansur

Sistan and
Baluchestan
(Iran)

Zaranj

Chahar Burjak

Chahar Burjak

Helmand

Helmand

Baluchistan
(Pakistan)

Table of Contents

List of Tables and Maps

Cover Photograph by Tech. Sgt. Laura Smith
Title Page Photograph by Romesh Bhattacharji

Acronyms and Key Terms

ABP	Afghan Border Police
ADT	Agribusiness Development Team
ANA	Afghan National Army
ANBP	Afghan National Border Police
ANDS	Afghan National Development Strategy
ANP	Afghan National Police
ANSF	Afghan National Security Forces
Arbakai	A volunteer, tribal police force which follows a strict ethical code
AWCC	Afghan Wireless Communication Company
BEFA	Basic Education for Afghanistan
BPHS	Basic Package of Health Services
CA	Civil Affairs
CDCs	Community Development Councils
CERP	Commander's Emergency Response Program
CHC	Comprehensive Health Centers
COIN	Counter Insurgency
CSO	Central Statistics Office
DDS	District Development Shuras
DIAG	Disbandment of Illegal Armed Groups
DoS	US Department of State
DST	District Support Team
FATA	Federally Administered Tribal Areas
GIRoA	Government of the Islamic Republic of Afghanistan
HIG or HIH	Hezb-e Islami Gulbuddin ("Islamic Party" formed by Gulbuddin Hekmatyar)
HIK	Hezb-e Islami Khalis ("Islamic Party" formed by Mohammad Yunus Khalis)

ICRC	International Committee of the Red Cross
IDLG	Independent Directorate for Local Governance
IED	Improvised Explosive Devices
IO	International Organization
IRoA	Islamic Republic of Afghanistan
ISAF	International Security Assistance Force
ISI	Inter-Service Intelligence (Pakistan)
Karez	A small underground irrigation system popular in Afghanistan
LGCD	Local Governance and Community Development Program
Meshrano Jirga	Elders' Assembly, upper house of Afghan National Assembly
MRRD	Ministry of Rural Rehabilitation and Development
Mustafiat	Department of Finance
NDS	National Directorate for Security
NGO	Non-Governmental Organization
NSP	National Solidarity Program
NWFP	North West Frontier Province
Pashtunwali	The Pashtuns' pre-Islamic code of conduct
PC	Provincial Council
PDC	Provincial Development Council
PDP	Provincial Development Plan
PRT	Provincial Reconstruction Team
UN	United Nations
UNAMA	United Nations Assistance Mission in Afghanistan
UNOPS	United Nations Office for Project Services
USACE	US Army Corp of Engineers
USAID	US Agency for International Development
USDA	US Department of Agriculture
Wali	Governor
Wolesi	Jirga People's Assembly, lower house of Afghan National Assembly
Woluswal	District Administrator

Guide to the Handbook

This handbook is a concise field guide to Nimroz for internationals deploying to the province. Field personnel have used these guides in Afghanistan since June 2008 to accelerate their orientation process and to serve as a refresher on different aspects of the province during their tour.

Reading this book will provide a basic understanding of the people, places, history, culture, politics, economy, needs, and ideas of Nimroz. Building upon this understanding can help you:

- Build rapport and a regular dialogue with local leaders.

- Plan and implement pragmatic strategies (security, political, economic) to address sources of instability.

- Influence communities to support the political process, not the insurgents.

- Build the capacity and legitimacy of a self-sufficient Afghan government and economy.

As you read the handbook and continue your inquiry in the province, seek to understand the influential leaders and groups in your local area and what beliefs and relationships drive their behavior. Think about the sources of violence in the area and whether groups are pursuing interests in a way that promotes conflict or stability. Finally, consider how various types of activities—key leader engagement, development assistance, security operations, security assistance, or public diplomacy—can effectively influence communities to work within the political process and oppose insurgency.

SOURCES AND METHODS

These handbooks are not intended as original academic research, but as concise, readable summaries for practitioners in the field. The editorial team relies on its collective field experience and knowledge of the province as well as key sources, such as the official Islamic Republic of Afghanistan (IRoA), United Nations, and United States Government (USG) publications, and those sources listed in the appendix.

The editors made every effort to ensure accuracy, but there is often considerable disagreement regarding what is "ground truth" in Nimroz and things are constantly changing. As such, consider this book part of your orientation, and not an all-inclusive source for everything you need to know.

Information in this handbook is unclassified. The views and opinions expressed in this handbook are those of IDS International and in no way reflect the views of the United States Government or the United States Army.

THE ELECTRONIC UPDATE

Look for electronic updates to this book at *www.idsinternational.net/ afpakbooks*. Updates will cover new developments, issues, and leaders that emerge after publication. They will also provide corrections and expanded content in key areas based on input from readers.

We hope the handbook will continue to be a valuable tool in thinking about the challenges in Nimroz. If you have questions, comments, or feedback for future updates or editions, please email *afpakbooks@ idsinternational.net*.

ABOUT IDS INTERNATIONAL

Publisher of Afghanistan and Pakistan Provincial Handbooks Series

This book is part of a series of handbooks on Afghanistan and Pakistan provinces and regions. Afghanistan province titles include Farah, Nuristan, Kunar, Nangarhar, Laghman, Khost, Paktika, Ghazni, Paktya, Helmand, Kandahar, and Nimroz. Pakistan province titles include North West Frontier Province (NWFP) and the Federally Administered Tribal Areas (FATA).

In addition to publishing these handbooks, IDS International provides training and analysis to government and private organizations in the areas of politics, economics, culture, stability operations, reconstruction, counterinsurgency, and interagency relations. In particular, IDS is a leading trainer of the US military in working with Provincial Reconstruction Teams (PRTs) in Iraq and Afghanistan. IDS offers its clients expertise and experience in the difficult work of interagency collaboration in complex operations. The writers and editors on this project offer a lifetime of experience working in these provinces and share a dedication to bringing peace and prosperity to the people of Afghanistan.

Authors: Richard M. Cavagnol and Sean Lockley
Editors: Nick Dowling and Saskia Funston
Assistant Editor: Tom Viehe
Reviewers: Gwen Cherne and Michael Rubin
Copy Editors: Michael Provenza, Emily Rose, and Gaye Newton

IDS INTERNATIONAL GOVERNMENT SERVICES

1916 Wilson Boulevard

Suite 302

Arlington, VA 22201

703-875-2212

www.idsinternational.net

afpakbooks@idsinternational.net

PUBLISHED: NOVEMBER 2010

This and other AfPak handbooks may be bought in either hard copy or digital format. Samples are available upon request. IDS International is also a leading provider of training and support on the cultural, political, economic, interagency and information aspects of conflict. For inquiries, please email afpakbooks@idsinternational.net or call 703-875-2212.

The village of Kace Satar outside the city of Delaram. While Nimroz is mostly desert, small settlements are scattered along the banks of the Khash Rod and Helmand Rivers. These waterways are the only sources of irrigation and drinking water in the province.

PHOTO BY JOBE SOLOMON

Chapter 1
Overview and Orientation

Nimroz is a sandy, sparsely inhabited wasteland. The desert of Dasht-e Margo sweeps across the landscape, broken up by roads that connect the people of the province to the rest of the country. Nimroz is part of the Sistan Basin, which encompasses large swaths of eastern Iran and southwestern Afghanistan. This basin stores water runoff from as far east as the Hindu Kush Mountains and helps sustain agriculture in the region. The province does not have many natural resources, such as minerals or timber. The Helmand River, Khash Rod River, and tributaries of the Farah River cut across this barren landscape and provide arable land on which people grow their crops. Both rivers meet in Kang district and flow into the Hamoon Saberi Lake which is shared between the Lash Wa Juwayn district of Farah province and Iran.

Agricultural land is located primarily along the Khash Rod and Helmand Rivers. Farming and livestock were the province's main sources of income, but severe droughts over the past five to seven years have taken their toll on the province. As a whole, the province suffers from poor irrigation and a lack of drinking water.

The majority of Nimrozi are Baluch and Pashtun, with a minority of Tajiks and Uzbeks. The Baluch are semi-nomads who wander across the province. The Pashtuns are more settled, working as farmers on the remaining arable land. The main Pashtun tribes are Durrani from the

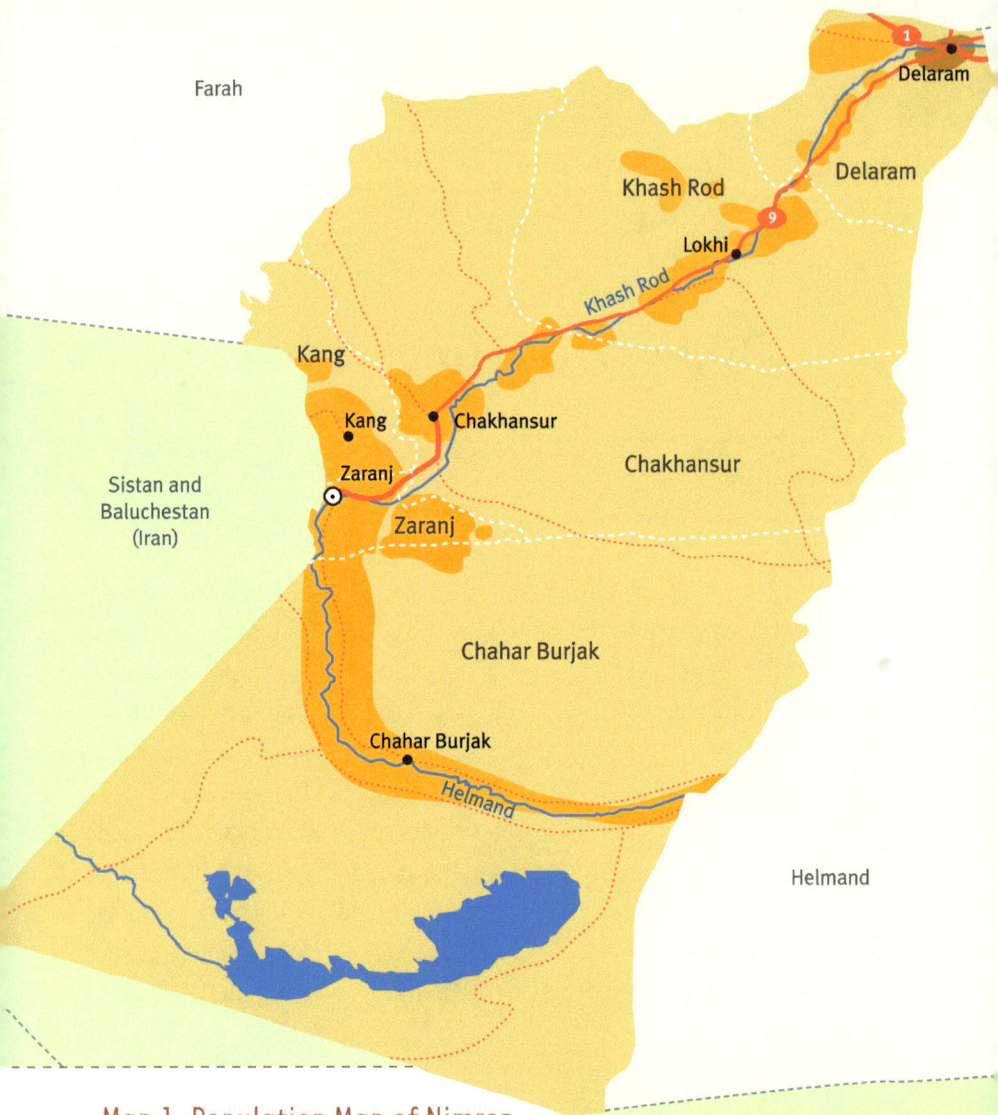

Map 1. Population Map of Nimroz

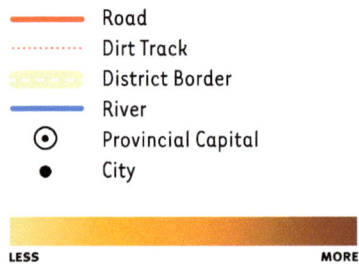

Farah

Khash Rod

Delaram

Delaram

Khash Rod

Lokhi

Kang

Kang

Chakhansur

Zaranj

Chakhansur

Zaranj

Sistan and
Baluchestan
(Iran)

Chahar Burjak

Chahar Burjak

Helmand

Helmand

Baluchistan
(Pakistan)

Legend	
Road	
Dirt Track	
District Border	
River	
Provincial Capital	
City	

LESS   MORE

Zirak and Panj-Pai sub-branches. The Barakzai and Noorzai are the two most prominent Pashtun tribes throughout the province.

Most of Nimroz is inaccessible to ISAF and the international community. Delaram district, located in the northeast corner of the province, has been the main focus of ISAF's efforts in the province. It is extremely difficult for ISAF troops and US government officials to travel to Zaranj, the province's capital, for security and political reasons. The main road, Route 9 or Route 606, runs from Delaram southwest to Zaranj. It is heavily mined and has many crossing points, known as "rat lines," for the Taliban moving east and west between Helmand province and Iran. Politically, Zaranj is within the ten kilometer zone of the Iranian border and requires special permission and extensive preparation for military and US government personnel to visit.

Despite these challenges, Nimroz has benefitted from having only three changes in the governor's office since 2001. Abdul Karim Brahui was the first governor after the fall of the Taliban and was re-appointed to the position in the fall of 2010. In the interim period, he remained close to President Karzai, serving his government in different positions.

ORIENTATION

Located in the southwest corner of Afghanistan, the province borders Iran to the west and Pakistan to the south. Within Afghanistan, Nimroz is bordered by Farah province to the north and Helmand province to the east. By area, Nimroz province is the fifth largest province in Afghanistan and one of the poorest. It covers an area of about 41,000 square kilometers with a topography that is mostly flat. Population estimates vary between 100,000 and 200,000 residents, with a 2004 Afghan Central Statistics Office census estimating that 149,000 people live in the province. This makes Nimroz the most sparsely populated province in the country. About 90 percent of the population lives in rural districts.

Table 1: District Populations

District	Center	Population	Tribes
Chahar Burjak	Chahar Burjak	4,180	Baluch, Durrani Pashtun
Chakhansur	Chakhansur	11,168	Baluch, Durrani Pashtun
Delaram	Delaram	16,000	Baluch, Noorzai Pashtun
Kang	Kang	13,514	Tajik, Baluch
Khash Rod	Lokhi	35,381	Brahui, Barakzai Pashtun
Zaranj	Zaranj	49,851	Baluch, Tajik
Total		130,094	

Source: CSO Provincial Profile

In the lower Sistan Basin, life depends on the inland delta of the Helmand River and the associated wetlands and lakes, the Hamoons. Water cover is extensive but shallow; the average depth of the Hamoons even at its highest does not exceed three meters. Wide but shallow lakes make for a system that is vulnerable to weather fluctuations and human interference of water flow, particularly since this very dry region has potential evaporation of more than three meters per year.

The delta has a positive effect on the local climate. The intensive evaporation decreases the enormous heat and humidity in the air. These wetlands make life possible in the region, providing a habitat for migrant and wintering waterfowl in the midst of the vast desert.

The Khash Rod and Helmand Rivers break up the vast desert. The Khash Rod River flows southwest, cutting across Khash Rod district from Delaram down to Zaranj. The Helmand River flows east from Helmand province west across Chahar Burjak district in southern Nimroz. The rivers often increase in depth and flow during the spring when the snow melts on the Hindu Kush Mountains. If precipitation levels are low, the Khash Rod River dwindles down to a trickle. There is very little rainfall throughout the year, so the farmers depend upon the Khash Rod River for irrigation of their fields.

Districts

Nimroz is divided into six districts: Chahar Burjak, Chakhansur, Kang, Khash Rod, Zaranj, and Delaram. The capital of Nimroz is the city of Zaranj in Zaranj district. Delaram is usually not included in demographic data because it was only recently added to Nimroz. It is unclear why the district was transferred from Farah province to Nimroz. Some have speculated that the addition of Delaram gave Nimroz greater access to provincial resources, strengthened tribal affinities, and allowed for greater financial income from customs revenue collected in Delaram from truck drivers and cargo carriers who do not have a stamp from the border crossing in Zaranj.

Key Towns

Located in the southwestern corner of the province, **Zaranj**, the capital of Nimroz, has a population of about 50,000. Zaranj lies on the traditional trade route between the Middle East, China, and India, and is situated next to the modern town of Milak, Iran. The city is clean, modern, and thriving, and benefits from extensive cross-border trade with Iran. In exchange for the unimpeded flow of the Khash Rod River from Afghanistan into Iran, Iran has also agreed to supply the city with electricity.

Delaram is the district center for the district of the same name. It is home to ISAF troops and a US government District Support Team (DST). Located along Route 1 (Ring Road) and at the conjunction of Route 522 to Gulistan district, Route 512 to Bakwa district, and Route 9 to Zaranj, Delaram is a major transportation hub for five provinces—Herat, Farah, Nimroz, Helmand, and Kandahar. Much of the produce sold in the large bazaar in Delaram comes from Farah City and Kandahar. The bazaar has become a trading hub for the surrounding districts, and merchants travel from other districts, provinces, and countries to buy and sell there.

RELEVANT HISTORICAL ISSUES

From Ancient to Modern Times

Around 1725 BC, Zarathushtra, a sage and distinguished mathematician and astronomer, set up an observatory in modern-day Nimroz province. He calculated that when the sun reached its highest point in the day over the Sistan, the entire eastern hemisphere would have daylight. He thus named that spot, 62 degrees longitude, the land of Nim Rouz, or "mid-day." In modern times, the province was known as Chakhansur province after a town in the province that served as a cultural hub along the Silk Road throughout medieval times. In 1968 it was renamed Nimroz province.

Present-day Nimroz was once part of the historical region of Sistan, where today the borders of Iran, Pakistan, and Afghanistan intersect. Over the centuries, Sistan was part of the Medean Empire, Alexander the Great's conquests, and the Kushan Empire before Arab invaders converted the region to Islam in the 7th century. Sparsely populated and largely inhospitable, Sistan provided a natural refuge for the early Kharijites, a violent dissident faction of Muslims who capitalized on anti-Arab sentiment and was responsible for assassinating Ali, the fourth Caliph, in 661.

Always a fairly wild region, in the ninth century, bandits and nomads harassed caravans and merchants traversing the region. With rebellions and unrest elsewhere in Islamic lands, the caliphate in Baghdad was stretched too thin to help restore order. Locals took matters into their own hands. A local coppersmith (*saffar* in Arabic) organized a militia which grew increasingly powerful, eventually leading to the creation of the Saffarid dynasty which dominated the region from the late ninth century to the first years of the 11th century. The Saffarids were among the first Iranian dynasties of the Islamic era.

The city of Zaranj was the capital of the Saffarid dynasty throughout the 9th century and remained one of the largest cities in the region. It was a cultural hub along the Silk Road until it was destroyed in 1383 by Timur (known in English as Tamerlane), who, like the Mongols before him, razed cities to strike fear into the conquered people.

After the destruction of Zaranj, Nimroz was relegated to a backwater on the periphery of, at various times, Iran's Safavid Empire and India's Mughal Empire. This has given the region cultural whiplash; the reality of power politics forced it to look culturally and politically both west and east in fairly quick succession. However, Mughal dominance preserved the region as largely Sunni after the Iranian government converted their lands to Shiism in the 16th century. Between 1870 and 1872, British tele-graph workers surveyed and demarcated what is now Iran's border with Afghanistan along Nimroz and Farah provinces. Iranian officials disagreed with the survey results, which they believed unjustly awarded Iranian territory to Afghanistan, but Iran in the late nineteenth century was too weak to do more than protest.

In 1970 the Afghan government rebuilt Zaranj, making it the capital of Nimroz province. Today, locals sometimes call it Shahr-e Naw, or "New City."

Communist Era (1979-1992)

In July 1973 Prime Minister Daoud overthrew his cousin, the king, and set himself up as the president of Afghanistan. During Daoud's short reign, the government began building a dam on the Helmand River in Chahar Burjak district, known as the Kamal Khan Dam. It was 50 percent complete when Daoud was overthrown by a communist coup in April 1978. The emergent Democratic Republic of Afghanistan (DRA) was poorly run by a faction-ridden Communist Party that alienated large sections of the populace. Work on the Kamal Khan Dam was stopped. To this day it remains incomplete largely due to pressure from Iran, which would receive less water from the Helmand River if it was dammed.

In December 1979 the Soviets invaded Afghanistan and quickly controlled the cities and government of Afghanistan. As in other provinces throughout Afghanistan, there were frequent skirmishes between local mujahedin and the Soviet 5th Division stationed in Herat. For example, in 1984 Mawlawi Mohideen Baluch set up a base about 10 kilometers south of Lokhi, the district capital of Khash Rod district along the Khash Rod River. From this base, he and his force of 200 mujahedin ambushed Soviet and DRA convoys traveling along Route 9 from Zaranj to Delaram. Despite numerical superiority and large numbers of armored vehicles, artillery, and aircraft, the Nimroz mujahedin were able to ambush the convoys, inflict serious casualties, destroy vehicles and equipment, and escape virtually unharmed.

In 1989 Soviet forces withdrew from Afghanistan. Three years later, the mujahedin succeeded in overthrowing the government.

Mujahedin and Taliban (1992-2001)

In 1992 Abdul Karim Brahui became governor of Nimroz, a post he held for three years before taking up arms against the Taliban. When the Taliban came to power in Herat, Ismail Khan, one of the key mujahedin leaders, drove the Taliban forces southeast and seized the town of Delaram (then in southwestern Farah). The Taliban agreed to leave Nimroz alone until it was clear who would hold power in Kabul. If the Taliban took Kabul, the mujahedin would turn over Nimroz without resistance. Only days later, however, the Taliban breached this agreement and invaded Nimroz. The mujahedin commander Abdul Karim Brahui (former governor of Nimroz) and his troops did not resist and withdrew to Iran.

The Taliban appointed Hamidullah Niyazmand as governor. Niyazmand was a descendent of the local Baluch Brahui tribe, the same tribe as Abdul Karim Brahui. Niyazmand knew and respected local customs and followed similar principles of governance as his predecessor. Nimroz inhabitants recount that the Taliban takeover led to the punishment of thieves and corrupt local officials instilling a perception of security and justice in the local population.

In the summer of 1995 the Taliban and Jamiat-e Islami (JI) fought for control of Delaram. After the Taliban conquest of Helmand in May 1995, the Taliban sought to secure Delaram as a stepping stone to advance further into Farah and Nimroz. By June the fighting was so intense that a rare ceasefire was mediated to remove bodies from the battlefield, tend to the wounded, and exchange prisoners. In August JI broke the cease-fire and mounted a major attack pushing Taliban forces back to Naw Zad in Helmand. While JI believed they had finally gained the upper hand, the Taliban quickly regrouped and mounted a counter-attack on Delaram in early September, isolating JI fighters in Helmand and Farah from their center of support in Herat City. The victory helped the Taliban seize Herat province on September 4, 1995.

The mujahedin briefly recaptured Zaranj in September 1995 and held it for several weeks. The Taliban quickly returned, seizing Herat in late 1995 and launching a new attack on Zaranj. Once again, the mujahedin leaders offered little resistance and fled to Iran. The new Taliban governors were seen as foreigners for their ties to Pakistan and their ignorance of local customs. Mullah Omar, the leader of the Taliban, supposedly issued a fatwa against the people of Nimroz, especially the Baluch and Shia population. Because the province was predominately Sunni, the fatwa amounted to a call for the ethnic cleansing of all non-Pashtuns.

The first of these new governors, Sher Malang, believed that the population was Shia—and thus heretics according to the Taliban—because of its proximity to Iran. Locals recall that.the governor had an order from the Taliban's central council to kill all males in Nimroz and marry off all females in order to cleanse the people of "unbelief," but there are no records of any mass executions or forced marriages in the province. Malang was replaced by Mullah Muhammad Rasul, who took control of the drug-smuggling in Nimroz, amassing a large fortune for himself at the expense of the local population. He later moved the capital of the province from Zaranj to the more Pashtun-populated town of Ghurghuri.

Under Taliban rule, Nimroz suffered a five year drought, stretching from 1997 to the winter of 2002. The drought hurt the economy as agriculture and livestock struggled to survive. The drought ended just a year after the Taliban's defeat, leading many to believe that it was divine punishment for the crimes of the Taliban and their rule.

Contemporary Events (2002-present)

When the US carried out airstrikes over Zaranj in November 2001, Governor Rasul and the Taliban fled the province. Abdul Karim Brahui was reappointed governor in 2002 and the province largely voted for Hamid Karzai in the 2004 presidential elections.

Since that time, however, the security situation has significantly deteriorated, with large portions of the province becoming inaccessible to ISAF and NGOs. As a result, US Marines set up a base in 2008 in the northeast corner of Nimroz province, near Delaram. This presence has provided a security backbone for the local Afghan National Army (ANA) and Afghan National Police (ANP) units in and around Delaram. The perceived improvement in security has helped to encourage an increased number of bazaar stalls.

Nevertheless, the security situation in Delaram is inconstant. In April 2009 the Afghan media reported a brief border skirmish between ANP and Iranian soldiers in which at least one Iranian was killed. The following month the Tehran-based Iranian news agency Tabnak accused the Afghan government and US forces of anti-Shia sectarian cleansing, a charge which appears to have had no basis in reality. In the fall of 2009 criminals began kidnapping people across the province for profit. In October 2009 residents of Delaram rioted in response to a Taliban accusation that US Marines had burned the Koran and had disrespected several women. This riot was quickly and peacefully quelled by a cooperative effort between several of the Delaram elders and the Marines.

In 2010 there was an increase in successful attacks against government officials. In January the mayor of Delaram was assassinated near the ANP station. In June nine suicide bombers attacked the provincial council and government buildings in Zaranj, killing one council member and several police and civilians. As a result the provincial council moved to Kabul for security reasons. The lack of a functioning provincial council has impacted the development of current Provincial Development Plans (PDPs) and it has made the provincial government even less accessible to the districts.

In late August 2010 Karzai removed Governor Azad and replaced him with former governor Abdul Karim Brahui. It is unclear what this will mean for the province, but many have speculated that the new governor will also be given a new set of ministers for the provincial government. From a district perspective such as that of Delaram, located 220 kilometers from Zaranj, this may be an improvement. Very little financial or resource support has been forthcoming from Zaranj and perhaps a change of government will improve the situation in the districts.

Afghan men speak with each other before the official start of a shura in Nimroz. Shuras are tribal meetings between elders to help address wrongs through arbitration and discussion. The term is now widely used to refer to any meeting between ISAF troops and Afghan leaders.

PHOTO BY CPL. ZACHARY J. NOLA

Chapter 2
Ethnicity, Tribes, Languages, and Religion

Afghan society is made up of interlocking and overlapping networks of affiliations, families, and occupations. Such a network is referred to as a *qawm*. Every individual belongs to a qawm, which provides cooperation, support, security, and assistance in social, political, or economic situations. Frequently a village corresponds to a qawm, which is more than a geographic location. In a more restricted sense, qawm refers to social groups, from family kin to ethnic group. In tribal areas qawm refers to a common genealogy from extended family or clan, to tribe or tribal confederation. Most simply, qawm defines an individual's identity in his social world.

ETHNICITY

The ethnic population of Nimroz is made up of Baluch, Pashtuns, Tajiks, and Uzbeks. The majority ethnic groups in Nimroz are Baluch and Pashtun. The Pashtuns are the largest and traditionally most politically powerful ethnic group in Afghanistan. They stretch across southern and eastern Afghanistan and into western Pakistan. Pashtuns are a tribal society made up of many tribal confederations, the largest being the Durrani and the Ghilzai. Most Pashtuns in Nimroz earn their living as farmers.

The Baluch are an Indo-Iranian ethnic group spread over Afghanistan, Pakistan, and Iran. Predominantly Sunni Muslim, in Afghanistan they are primarily nomadic, roaming the Chahar Burjak district of Nimroz. These semi-sedentary and semi-nomadic populations are famed for camel breeding. They number around 100,000, although other estimates are lower. Like the Pashtuns, the Baluch are comprised of several different tribes.

The Baluch occupy the southern part of Nimroz province and are concentrated around the capital, Zaranj. Because international borders often do not coincide with tribal borders, the Baluch maintain close cross-border family ties with each other. There is considerable cross-border movement of the Baluchs between Afghanistan, Iran, and Pakistan's Baluchistan province. Many of them have identity cards from Afghanistan and Iran as well as Pakistani documents, which allow them to cross the border easily and almost without restriction.

LANGUAGES

Dari is the main language of the government in Nimroz. It is closely related to the Farsi spoken in Iran, and the two—along with Tajik—are sometimes categorized as dialects of Persian rather than separate languages. Modern Persian is an Indo-European language, more closely related to French than to Arabic. Nevertheless, just as English has words with both Latin and Germanic origin, modern Persian is a mix between words rooted in the Old Persian of the ancient Achaemenid Empire and Arabic vocabulary adopted after the seventh century Arabic invasion. Baluchi, more widely spoken, serves as the language in everyday communication.

The languages people speak often correspond to their ethnicity and role in society. The Baluch speak Baluchi, Pashtuns speak Pashto, and Tajiks often speak Dari. Baluchi is spoken by about 60 percent of the population, mostly concentrated in the south and northwest of the province. Pashto is spoken by 27 percent of the population, primarily in the rural areas and across the central, northern, and northeastern regions. Dari and Uzbek speakers account for 10 percent of the population each, and a moderate population of Tajik speakers exist in Zaranj. They speak various Tajik dialects of Dari.

ROLE OF TRIBES

The tribe is the most powerful structure of Pashtun society and provides an informal governance structure. There is some disagreement among scholars as to whether these structures are "tribes" according to the Middle Eastern definition. In keeping with common usage, these structures will be referred to as "tribes" throughout this book.

Overarching decisions affecting the tribe are made at the tribal level. Tribal society works on a group rather than an individual decision-making structure. All decisions for the tribe or sub-tribe are determined as a group by *maliks,* the tribal elders. In the tribe, the goal of the justice system is the promotion of group harmony and consensus rather than the administration of corporal punishment to the individual.

There are two primary mechanisms for tribal elders to make decisions. The first is a *jirga*—a meeting held to make a specific decision. It can involve people from within or outside the tribe. Any decision made by the jirga is considered binding.

The second meeting type is the *shura*, from the Arabic word for "consultation." Shuras provide a mechanism for correcting wrongs through arbitration and discussion. The focus is more on soothing bruised egos, addressing issues of pride, and negotiating compensation rather than imposing punishments. After decades of war, shuras have become advisory councils that can include elders, commanders, and landowners *(khans)* to address issues of security and rule of law. Recently, the term

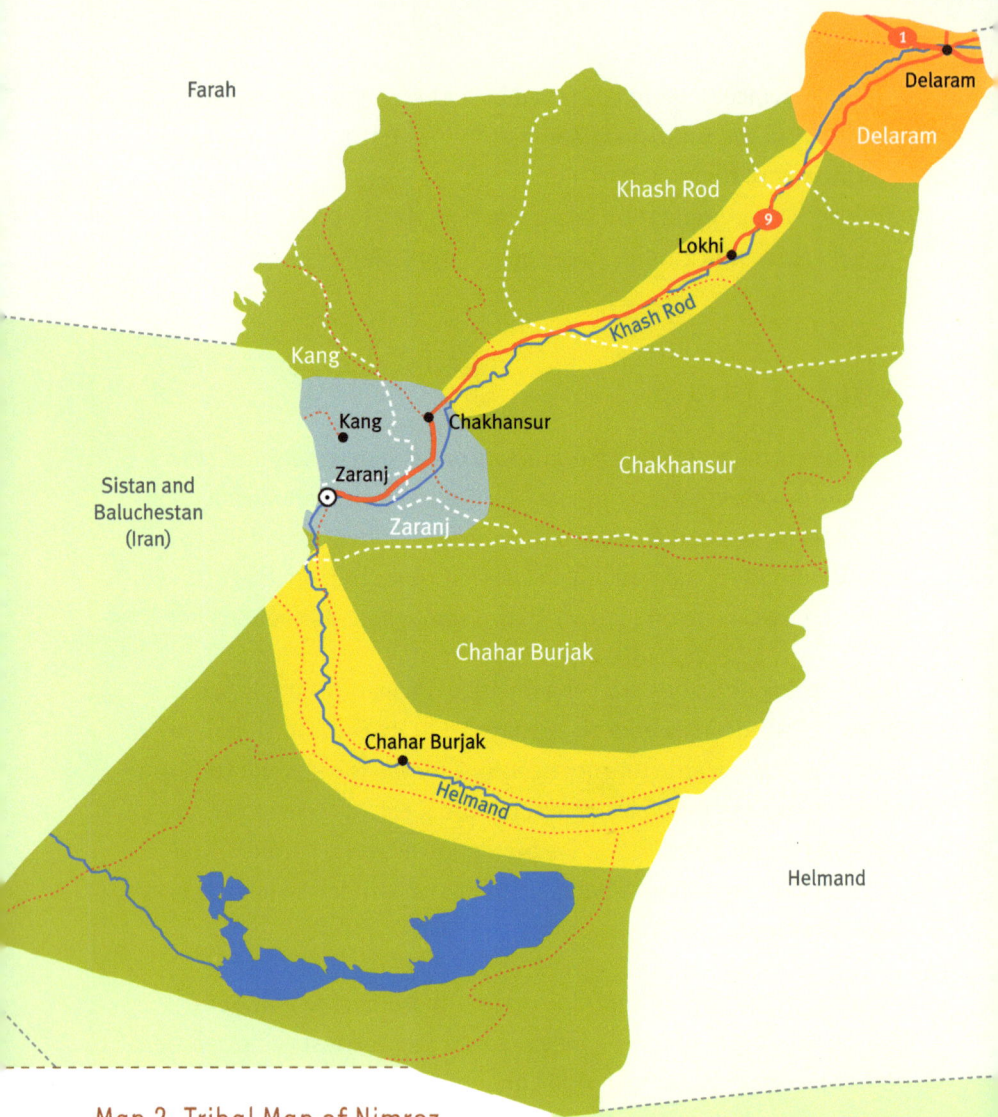

Map 2. Tribal Map of Nimroz

Legend:
- Road
- Dirt Track
- District Border
- River
- Provincial Capital
- City
- Baluch
- Mixed Durrani Pashtun
- Tajik
- Noorzai

Labels on map:
- Farah
- Delaram
- Delaram
- Khash Rod
- Khash Rod
- Lokhi
- 1
- 9
- Kang
- Kang
- Chakhansur
- Chakhansur
- Zaranj
- Zarani
- Sistan and Baluchestan (Iran)
- Chahar Burjak
- Chahar Burjak
- Helmand
- Helmand
- Baluchistan (Pakistan)

shura has been used to refer to any meeting between ISAF troops and Afghan counterparts to discuss mutual issues.

In the Baluch tribes, much like the Pashtun tribes, the decision-making power lies with the tribal elders. The tribal leader of a Baluch tribe—the *sardar*—has immense powers and can make decisions in consultation with sectional chiefs (*hakims*) of the tribe. Sardars are elected and are supported by the people of the tribe who often give a double share of tribal land to the sardar to support his position.

The tribal structure is based on feudal-type relationships between the hakims and their followers, which may include low-level leaders, tenant farmers, and descendants of former slaves (*hizmatkar)*. The hakim maintains this hierarchal relationship by offering money, and in the case of war, the spoils. Like those who follow pashtunwali, Baluchs are strong supporters of personal honor, open hospitality, and a willingness to provide help and assistance to all who need it.

The Baluch consider a woman a full partner in all social endeavors with recognized rights and privileges. She is treated as an equal and is accorded a position of trust and confidence. She is neither veiled nor treated as a second-class citizen. She may own and inherit property. In addition to performing the normal household chores, the woman also takes part in manly occupations, such as grazing flocks and assisting in cultivation.

Disputes between individuals or groups are arbitrated through a *Medh o Maraka*. The wronged party in the dispute, such as a blood feud or robbery, is contacted and asked to agree to a Medh. A jirga of important village personalities then goes to the house of the offended party and accepts forgiveness from the offender for the wrongdoing, offering unconditional apologies to the offended party. The offended party accepts the apologies and the matter is closed. If the offended party does not agree to the Medh o Maraka, the issue is settled by a jirga with blood-for-blood consequences for the offending party.

Pashtunwali

Society in Nimroz is very conservative, strictly religious, and struc-
tured around *pashtunwali,* meaning "the way of the Pashtuns." This
is a pre-Islamic legal and moral code that determines social order and
responsibilities. It contains sets of values pertaining to honor, solidarity, hospitality, mutual support, shame, and revenge. The founda-
tion of the Pashtun social order, these values define the individual
responsibilities of each Pashtun to his Muslim faith. The defense of
honor, even unto death, is obligatory for every Pashtun. All Pashtuns
have some knowledge of the code and will try to follow it. Some
tribes are stricter about the code than others. The five main tenets of
pashtunwali are as follows:

Nang (Honor): All parts of pashtunwali lead to honor. All Pashtuns
are required to uphold the honor of their family and their tribe by
following the other parts of the code. An insult to someone's tribe or
family can lead to Badal (see below). The biggest disputes are over
women, land, and money. A Pashtun man must protect all three with
his life and honor.

Melmastia (Hospitality): Pashtuns are known for their hospitality and
will go to great lengths to treat their guest with honor and respect.
Most villages and large families will have a dedicated guesthouse.
Even if a family has limited resources, a stranger will still be welcomed,
fed, and given a place to sleep. This applies to non-Pashtuns as well.

Nanawatay (Sanctuary): If one Pashtun has insulted or committed a
crime against another, they are allowed to admit their guilt and ask
for forgiveness. They will take gifts to the offended party and ask that
the past be forgotten. The insulted party is then obligated to accept
their offer. Often the women of a family or tribe will arrange for this to
happen because women are seen as natural peacemakers. Nanawatay
can also be used to beg for mercy and protection.

Badal (Revenge): Pashtuns are quick to take revenge for an insult or seek justice for a past crime. It does not matter if the insult is decades old. The only way to restore honor to one's family/clan/tribe is to exact revenge on the other's family/clan/tribe.

Namus (Honor of Women): Pashtuns defend the honor of Pashtun women from verbal and physical harm at all costs.

Predominant Tribes in Nimroz

The Pashtun tribes in Nimroz belong to the Durrani confederation or "super-tribe." Many prominent leaders from Afghan history have come from the Durrani confederation, including the royal family, bureaucrats, businessmen, and high ranking military leaders. Because the Durrani are often associated with the leaders of Afghanistan, they are seen as oppressors by other super-tribes, such as the Ghilzai.

Categorizing Pashtuns is a bit abstract to most Nimrozi. Nobody would describe themselves as "Durrani." Instead, they would always use their specific tribal name, such as Noorzai. Even smaller divisions within the tribes can be politically important. Some tribes divide along clan lines over whether they support or oppose the government.

The map on page 16 shows which tribes are predominant in broad swaths of the province, but this information should be used with caution. Tribes are scattered across Nimroz in a dense patchwork, dividing districts—and even villages—into distinct zones of control. Rival tribes can hold sway over neighboring clusters of houses in the same town.

The primary Pashtun tribe in Nimroz is the **Noorzai,** which accounts for about 67 percent of the population. The subtribes of the Noorzai include the Jamalzai, Khochezai, Walarzai, Elaizai, Smailzai, Jendan, Chagazai, Aghakhel, Tamanian, and Sagzai. While often considered members of the Durrani super-tribe, many Zirak Durranis dismiss

Table 2: Major Tribes in Nimroz

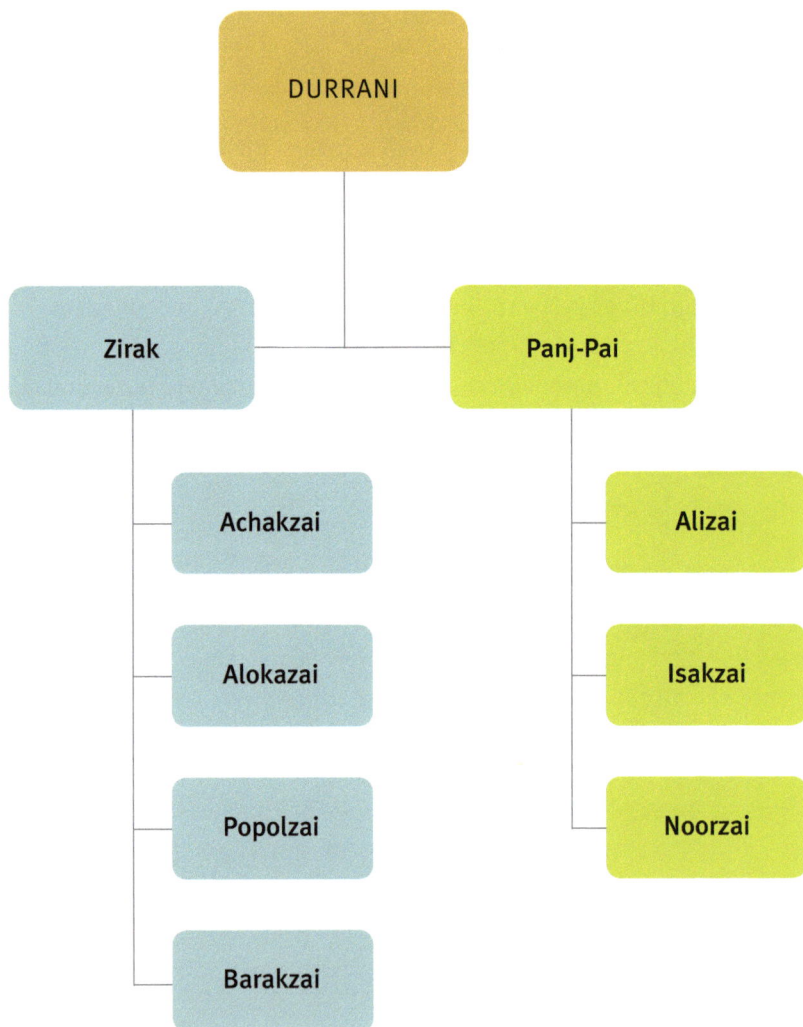

the Noorzai as Ghilzai because of their close relationship with the Ghilzai-dominated Taliban leadership over the past three decades. Given the numbers and importance of the Noorzai in Nimroz, this attitude may have consequences for long-term politics.

The **Barakzai**, the most important subtribe of the Zirak tribe in Nimroz, constitutes about 23 percent of the Nimroz population. Other sub-tribes include the Achakzai, Alokazai, Mohammadzai, and Popolzai. All Zirak subtribes are Durrani Pashtuns, but the Barakzai have furnished a string of kings to the monarchy of Afghanistan. They are one of the most respected tribes in the country.

The **Kuchi** are Pashtun nomads. They are thought of as a caste of nomadic herdsmen who care for sheep, goats, camels, and donkeys. They are able to cross boundaries with ease and are strong ideological supporters of the Taliban. It is estimated that there are 30,000 Kuchi in Nimroz.

ROLE OF RELIGION

Islam is a central, pervasive influence throughout Afghan society and is totally intertwined with the activities of each day. The Afghan constitution states explicitly that no laws will be enacted that contradict Sharia law. The mullahs also play a role in village legal proceedings, thus further intertwining religion, law, and governance. Individual and family status depends on the proper observance of the society's value system based on concepts defined in Islam. These are characterized by honesty, frugality, generosity, virtuousness, piousness, fairness, truthfulness, tolerance, and respect for others. The prevailing religion of the Baluch who live in Nimroz is the Hanafi school of Sunni Islam, making it the main religion in the province. There is also a small percentage of Shia Muslims in the province.

The mosque is the center of religious life in rural Nimroz province. It is both a holy place and a communal center. Smaller community-maintained mosques stand at the center of villages as well as town and city neighborhoods. Indeed, the size of a village is often described by the number of mosques it has. Zaranj has two Jameh (congregational) mosques with capacities of 400 and 150, respectively. Delaram is populated by a number of smaller mosques that have sprung up as communities of internally displaced persons (IDPs) settle in and around the city center.

Mosques serve not only as places of worship, but as a shelter for guests, a place to meet and gossip, the focus of social religious festivities, and schools. Almost every Afghan has studied at a mosque school or madrassa. For many, especially in rural Nimroz, this is the only formal education they receive. There is no madrassa in Delaram; rather, the mullahs teach young men in their homes or a mosque.

The mullah is the spiritual leader of the village and traditionally settles disputes like a judge and plays the role of a teacher in the absence of a formal education system in the village. Some are barely literate, or only slightly more educated than the people they serve. Mullahs are normally appointed by the government after consultation with their communities and, although partially financed by the government, mullahs are largely dependent on community contributions for their livelihood, including shelter and a portion of the harvest. Supposedly versed in the Koran, Sunna, Hadith, and Sharia, they are charged with teaching the members of their community the fundamentals of Islamic ritual and behavior. They often take positions on political issues. When discussing the power of the mullahs, a district governor in Nimroz province once remarked, "If I say to the people 'do X' and the mullahs say 'do Y,' the people will do Y."

In Delaram and in the surrounding small villages where there is little government influence, people come to the mullahs to arbitrate disputes. The mullahs address their questions to religious scholars who consult religious texts before recommending a resolution. Disputes range from the mundane (shop disputes and family issues) to the significant (land disputes and rules of warfare).

On February 20, 2010, US Marines in Delaram convened a religious shura at the district governor's office in Delaram. It was attended by nine key mullahs from Delaram. Among those in attendance was Maulawi Abdul Bari, a former imam at Jameh mosque in Delaram and the senior, most influential mullah in Delaram. The mullahs and religious scholars (maulawis) of Delaram appear to have no formal relationship with the provincial Director of Haj and Religious Affairs, with whom they engaged during the lottery for the Haj, or with the Ulema Council located in the capital of Zaranj. The Ulema Council is the central body of religious scholars who ostensibly advise the government and country's religious network. As with previous mullah engagements, these mullahs referred to the Taliban as "outsiders" and foreigners and thus claimed to have little influence over them.

Asadullah Haqdost, the district governor of Delaram (center), speaks with officials a boys' school. Tensions and disputes between local and provincial government officials are common and can negatively impact local governance.

PHOTO BY SGT. DORIAN GARDNER

Chapter 3
Government and Leadership

Governance in Nimroz faces challenges of insecurity, corruption, poor public health, illegal or unauthorized settlements, and lack of employment. District administrations have trouble maintaining a staff, particularly in professional positions. Many of the towns and villages of Nimroz have less than a ten percent literacy rate. As a result, government positions, such as judge, prosecutor, lawyer, district directors of the various ministries, and others must be drawn from large population centers, such as Zaranj, Kandahar, Herat, and Kabul.

HOW THE GOVERNMENT OFFICIALLY WORKS

Central Control

Authority and power in Afghanistan are concentrated in the national government as a means to counter the power of warlords in the provinces. As such, the provincial government is limited to an advisory role for the central government, while decisions on everything from policy to funding priorities are made in Kabul.

Provincial Government

A governor *(wali)* heads the provincial government and reports to the Independent Directorate for Local Governance (IDLG) located in the Executive Office of the president. A deputy and several staff assist him to oversee provincial government management.

Ministries in Kabul execute their policies and programs through departments at the provincial level. Ministers, with the approval of the president, appoint provincial directors who manage these departments. The director reports to and receives funds from the ministry in Kabul. The governor does not have budgetary authority over any of these departments but must approve all expenditures before they are processed by the Department of Finance *(Mustafiat)*.

The Provincial Council (PC), the elected body at the provincial level, provides a voice for the people on provincial issues. The PC reports directly to the president and has no budget. Its relevance is largely dependent on the governor's support and its members' individual resources and initiatives.

The Provincial Development Committee (PDC), including the governor and department heads, is responsible for creating the Provincial Development Plan (PDP) and coordinating with key players on development needs. External players such as the UN, PRT, and interested NGOs also attend meetings.

District and Local Governance

Government at the district level mirrors the provincial government with the district administrator or sub-governor *(woluswali)*, police chief, National Directorate of Security officer, clerks, and a small police force. The district governor or district sub-governor *(woluswali)* is

Table 3: Provincial Line Directors and Provincial Government Officials

Title Of Duty	Name
Provincial Governor	Abdul Karim Brahui
Deputy Governor	Malang Rasoli
Head of Provincial Court	Faqir Ahmad
Provincial Chief of Police	Jabar Purdill
Provincial Border Police Chief	Ghulam Haidar
Head of NDS	Sadullah
Director of Rural Reconstruction	Engineer Khali
Director of Agriculture	Mohd Akbar
Director of Water Management	Haji Sharwali
Director of Education	Khalilullah
Director of Refugees & Returnees	Amanullah Sultani
Director of Communications	Juraludeen
Director of Public Health	Dr. Noor Ahamad
Director of Power and Electricity	Zmarai
Director of Public Works	Habibullah

Provincial Council

Provincial Council	
Provincial Council	Sardar Abdul Razaq
Provincial Council	Mohammad Sidiq
Provincial Council	Gul Ahmad Ahmadi
Provincial Council	Haji Sayyad Ahmad
Provincial Council	Khudaidad
Provincial Council	Haji Sakhi Ahmad
Provincial Council	Rooh Gul Khairzad
Provincial Council	Gul Makai Wakili
Provincial Council	Shakila Hakimi

NOTE: The most common way to reach government officials in Nimroz province is by cell phone. For a list of up-to-date numbers, contact the District Support Team (DST) in Delaram.

appointed by the president with concurrence of the provincial governor. The district governor comes under the formal control of the provincial governor. Ministry sub-departments also operate at the district level, but are not present in every district.

Under the current centralized fiscal structure, the provinces and districts function as collectors of revenue from various, often undefined, sources that they send to the central government for inclusion in the national budget. The province is in turn funded by transfers from the central government, while the districts are funded by provincial transfers. In 2007 District Development Assemblies (DDAs) were formed in order to plan, prioritize, and coordinate development activities at the district level. Below the district level, the only formal governance structures are the Community Development Councils (CDCs). These CDCs help the Ministry of Rural Rehabilitation and Development (MRRD) manage the National Solidarity Program.

Some villages have set up CDCs under the National Solidarity Program. The CDC is responsible for prioritizing and articulating the development needs of the community to the Afghan government and the international donor community. The CDC is elected by the villagers and the council itself generally appoints a leader (*raees shora-e enkeshafi*), an official position recognized by the government. The position of CDC head may or may not be influential, depending on the individual occupying the post. Many times another leader, such as a malik or zamindar, will be appointed to this post, in which case the position allows him to consolidate his influence.

Municipalities are governance structures that work independently from provincial and district governance. The municipality of Zaranj is led by a mayor appointed by the president in consultation with the governor. Municipalities and the mayors who run them do not come under the formal control of the provincial governor in the provinces in which they reside. Municipalities are required by law to raise revenue from local sources and sustain their operations and services entirely out of such revenues. Municipalities, independent from the provincial government, are free to plan, fund, and implement projects, and tax local businesses.

HOW IT ACTUALLY WORKS

While the provincial government structure is theoretically formalized, most sub-national structures are ad hoc constructs, frequently reflecting personal relationships. In addition to the formal structures, informal community shuras, jirgas, and other traditional structures remain influential at the local level. These traditional structures are part of the fabric of Afghan culture and must seamlessly align within the provincial structure for effective governance.

Disputes between local and provincial officials are common and have a significant impact on governance. For example, the provincial government in Delaram has given very little support to the district government. Asadullah Haqdost was appointed district governor in November 2009 and has been governing Delaram without a *tashkil*— official authorization—for a specific number of government funded posts. In January 2010 he requested a judge, prosecutor, deputy district governor, administrative assistant, and tribal council administrator from then-Governor Azad. As of October 2010, none of these positions have been filled, and there has been one visit in nine months from the provincial governor and provincial line ministries.

In January 2010 about 450 elders of Delaram gathered and selected a 42-member community council to work with and act as a check and balance for the district governor. One member from each of the 21 villages surrounding Delaram was selected to represent the interests of the rural population. Similarly, 21 representatives from the Delaram district center were selected to represent the interests of the urban population, especially the owners of the bazaar shops. While this group has met infrequently and could use training in basic governance from the Independent Directorate of Local Governance (IDLG), they were able to produce a prioritized list of development projects for the urban and rural communities. The next step is to elect a formal Community Development Council (CDC) to develop a District Development Plan (DDP) that will be sent to the Provincial Council for incorporation into the Provincial Development Plan (PDP).

Corruption in Nimroz's provincial and district governments is common. Officials take bribes, extort money from shop owners and contractors building coalition bases, and facilitate the transport of narcotics. This type of corruption affects nearly every program and revenue-generating project. Unfortunately, it is difficult to prove specific incidents of corruption; officials are reluctant to charge each other publically.

Village Governance

In the rural areas, Afghan villages are defined less by their geographic boundaries and more by a strong sense of community and belonging. Rural villages are essentially clusters of independent families. The village may go by different names depending upon whom one asks. It may be named after someone significant in the village, in which case the name may be changed when that person dies. Villages often have minimal government presence.

There are five types of Afghan village leadership and supporting leadership positions: political, economic, religious, tribal, and military. Not every village will have each type of leader, and there may be more than one leader in each category. Some terms such as malik and khan are used generically to mean "leader" and can cause confusion.

Political Leadership: The *malik* is the village representative to the state. He will interact with district and provincial officials and officials from international NGOs or coalition forces. A malik is often elected or appointed by villagers, who pay him for his services.

Economic Leadership: In an agricultural community, the *arbabs*, *zamindars,* or *khans* are the landholders or landlords. These positions are found more often in southern Afghanistan, where larger landholdings are common. These landlords are the chief employers and drivers of the villages' economy. In addition to providing the economic backbone of the village, the economic leader also provides some basic community services, such as a salary for the village mullah, following customary cultural guidelines of generosity.

Religious Leadership: Each village will probably have at least one *mullah*. Village mullahs play an extremely important role in the community. They preside at births, weddings, deaths, and other significant societal events. Depending on the size or isolation of the village, a mullah may also be the only teacher, dispenser of folk medicine, or legal authority. Different ethnic or tribal cliques (qawms) may opt to have their own mullahs.

Tribal Leadership: The true tribal leader, known as the *khan* or *mesher,* is not generally considered part of the village leadership, as his focus is more on the function of the tribe. His sphere of influence may encompass several villages. However, the tribal leader does have influence on his tribe's activities in a village. If a tribal leader does reside in a particular village, his responsibility and influence will certainly extend beyond it.

The tribal leader is not the same as one of the local village elders (see below), although he most likely engages with the local elders in order to understand the local situation. The collective tribal, clan, or village leadership institutions—the jirga or shura—connect the local village leaders with the larger tribal qawm led by the tribal leader.

The position of tribal leader may or may not be a powerful one, depending on the cohesiveness of the tribe, its size, its wealth, the personality of the tribal leader, and other factors.

Military Leadership: Some villages may have a military commander, known as the *qomandan* or *komandan*. This commander may have variable prominence within the village hierarchy. A powerful qomandan may become a local warlord. After the anti-Soviet jihad, qomandans and their desire to gain more power and revenue was one factor that led to the Afghan civil war. This recent memory is one reason why a strong commander or permanent position of military commander may not be welcomed by all residents and current power holders.

Supporting Leadership Roles

Other additional positions may have a degree of power or influence depending on local situations. Supporting leadership roles in villages vary region to region and village to village. The following list of known supporting roles is not exhaustive, but it indicates what each position involves.

Mohasen safid (village elders) are the "white beard" or "grey beard" men of the village who offer their wisdom in collective jirgas or shuras and mediate conflicts between other village leaders and powerbrokers. Their authority is not formal, but their power comes from their ability to influence other powerbrokers.

The **mirab (village water manager)** manages the village water supply, resolves disputes about water resources, and helps plan the agricultural economy of the village.

Appointed by the zamindar, the **chak bashi (village agricultural specialist)** works closely with farmers to coordinate agricultural activities in the area.

Other villagers may have some unofficial status as leaders, due to their professions (teachers or doctors), education, or perceived worldliness. Villagers may have these people engage with outsiders, but they are probably not the key leaders or decision makers themselves.

Titles of respect are abundant in Afghanistan. Engineer, Maulawi, Haji, and Sayed are all titles of respect that many people will place in front of their names. These titles are not reserved for people who are leaders or experts. They are honorific titles. As a sign of respect to the title holder, people may often defer to those with titles during discussions. Engineer is a title granted to people who have received an engineering degree, Maulawi is given to Sunni Muslim scholars, Haji is reserved for those who have completed the Haj (pilgrimage) to Mecca, and Sayed is reserved for men who are recognized as being descendents of the Prophet Muhammad.

SECURITY FORCES

Afghan National Army (ANA)

Afghan National Security Forces (ANSF) are weak in Nimroz, especially in the Delaram area. There are two Afghan National Army (ANA) *kandaks* (battalions) and the 215 Corps HQ on station at Forward Operating Base (FOB) Delaram. In the past, the Marines have had little or no involvement with the ANA, and they did not conduct joint patrols or operations. This may change with the addition of the Georgian forces to Delaram. The ANA is respected and trusted by the local population.

Afghan Highway Patrol (AHP)

The Afghan Highway Police (AHP) was originally tasked with manning checkpoints along the major roads in Afghanistan. In many areas, the AHP was using these checkpoints to unlawfully tax motorists and truck drivers. During the past several years, the Afghan Highway Patrol (AHP) has been disbanded throughout most of Afghanistan. But the leadership and patrolmen that operate in Delaram district have not disbanded, and they continue to report to a general in Herat province. The now defunct AHP continues to operate along Route 9 despite having no sanction from the Ministry of Interior. Provincial officials and the Ministry of the Interior have been calling for the consolidation of the ANP and AHP, but the general in Herat is reluctant to give up the revenue of illegal customs that AHP collects for him.

Afghan National Police (ANP)

The Afghan National Police (ANP) is operational throughout Nimroz and is of generally poor to marginal quality. In Delaram, it is in charge of security inside city limits. In Delaram, there is one police unit with about 30 police officers at the ANP HQ where a platoon of US Marines, a civilian-led police mentoring team (PMT), and a District Support Team (DST) are located, along with the district government center which houses the district governor and his security team.

Civilians have a neutral to negative view of the police. The ANP has a reputation for stealing money from the people. Typical challenges facing the police have been weak leadership, extortion of the population, drug use, and incompetence. Some of these problems remain even after the police cohort has gone through designated training programs. Often the cause of the problem is that the police are not being paid and feel they have no recourse other than to take money from the population.

Most of the ANP working in Delaram have family in other provinces. The primary language of the ANP is Dari while the local population speaks Pashto. The police reportedly patrol the bazaar and surrounding areas twice a day and only when accompanied by Marines. Many of the ANP patrolmen do not feel they have the training or equipment to survive an attack against insurgent forces. In mid-2010 ANP troops attended a 60-day training program at Camp Leatherneck. The returning graduates appear to be motivated and have developed a more professional attitude than the untrained officers.

Afghan Border Police (ABP)

The Afghan Border Police (ABP) is responsible for border security along the Nimroz borders with Iran and Pakistan. In general, it is poorly trained and led, and its policemen are reluctant to patrol except when accompanied by US Marines. But many ABP officers help narcotics traffickers. This collusion is probably the result of the geographic isolation of Nimroz and its limited connections to the central government. In an effort to improve the quality of the ABP, an ongoing United Nations Office on Drugs and Crime (UNODC) project has provided radio communication equipment, vehicles, and narcotics identification kits to 25 border posts in Herat, Farah, and Nimroz. The construction of a Regional Logistic and Maintenance Unit in Nimroz is underway.

Table 4: Nimroz District Sub-governors

Name	District Name
Khoda Nazar	Chahar Burjak
Haji Aqa M.	Chakhansur
Ghulam Sarwar Sherzad	Kang
M. Hashem	Khash Rod
N/A	Zaranj
Asadullah Haqdost	Delaram

LEADER PROFILES

Abdul Karim Brahui (sometimes spelled Brahawi), Governor: Brahui was appointed governor of Nimroz immediately after the fall of the Taliban due to his strong ties to Baluch tribes in the province. During this time, he strengthened his links to local smuggling networks, particularly with his cousin Haji Juma Khan Mohammadhasni. Persistent claims that he was involved in illicit activity led to his removal in December 2004. Nevertheless, President Karzai remained eager to keep the support of the Baluch, keeping Brahui involved in his government. In 2010 Karzai made Brahui governor of Nimroz again, replacing Dr. Ghulam Dastagir Azad.

Karim Brahui is not an ethnic Baluch, but is from a tribe assimilated by the Baluch that continues to use its own political structure and language. Brahui is from Nimroz, where he graduated from Cadet School in 1973. After a short military career in Kabul, Brahui returned to Nimroz in 1979 to defend his home against the Soviets. Brahui fortified his local standing when he fought the Taliban in the 1990s alongside Ismail Khan, although Nimroz did fall in late February 1995.

During the Taliban administration, Brahui lived in Zahedan in Iran. He is suspected of cultivating links to Iran's intelligence services during the Soviet occupation and a number of his family members have possibly settled in Sistan & Baluchistan province. Despite his exile, Brahui continued to wield influence in Nimroz through his position as a prominent Baluch and his relationship with the Iranians. Brahui became involved in smuggling activity during this period.

Asadullah Haqdost, Delaram District Governor: The previous provincial governor, Dr. Azad, appointed Asadullah Haqdost as the Delaram District Governor (DG) in late 2009, replacing Ismail Khan. Haqdost is 57 years old in 2010 and was born in the village of Hoaja in Bakwa district. Haqdost is a Noorzai from the Dirruzai sub-tribe and has lived in Nimroz for the past 17 years. Haqdost held a variety of government positions between 1977 and 1989. He moved to Zaranj around 1992 and held several positions in the provincial government until his appointment as district governor in 2009.

Asadullah Haqdost is a forward-thinking district governor who has prodded the Community Council to meet and put forth a prioritized list of community projects that can be funded by CERP and USAID to better the community and put people to work. He is aggressive in pursuing insurgents that attempt to infiltrate Delaram and has been an advocate of checkpoints along the major routes to discourage the entry of insurgents and capture insurgents fleeing Delaram after an incident.

The DG has worked closely with the DST and the CAG to stimulate the economy through projects and has tried to initiate funding and training for women-owned and operated businesses. Well liked and respected by the population, he has developed and maintained cordial relations with the Marines.

Noor Alah, Mayor of Delaram: District Governor Asadullah Haqdost appointed Noor Alah as the Mayor of Delaram after the assassination of Abdullah Jan in January 2010. He was born and raised in Washer, a nearby district of Helmand province. Noor Alah moved with his father and six brothers to Lashkar Gah. When former District Governor Ismael Khan asked him to move to Delaram, he did so with three of his brothers. Noor Alah's primary duties include managing all aspects of the Delaram bazaar. There have been reports that he and his body guards extort money from shopkeepers.

Colonel Abdul Qadus, Delaram District Chief of Police: Colonel Qadus was appointed the ANP Chief on March 14, 2009. With 28 years on the force, he has held several posts, including the head of the Farah Prison, and various undercover assignments. His wife is a provincial council member of Farah province. During a meeting in January 2009 with local elders, he emphasized that he and his men could not secure the city themselves, but would need the help of all the citizens of Delaram. Many felt at that time that he was lazy and the general population had little faith in the ANP.

Colonel Qadus has improved the effectiveness of his police force. Locals are beginning to trust the ANP, and in October 2009 they took the lead in quelling a violent demonstration. Clearly there is still a long way to go before the ANP in Nimroz become a trusted citizen-centered police force able to instill confidence in the population.

Abdul Khaliq, Delaram District Development Director: In August 2009 the Nimroz provincial governor appointed Abdul Khaliq the Delaram District Development Committee Chairman (DDDCC) to oversee and assist in the development of projects for the Delaram district center. Abdul Khaliq is a Noorzai from the Chagazai sub-tribe and resides in Kace Satar. It is believed that he was appointed as the DDDCC because of his extensive schooling, knowledge of the contracting business, and personal wealth (it is reported that he owns as many as 250 shops in the bazaar).

In addition to being the DDDCC, Abdul Khaliq is the vice president of a construction company located in Herat. He is an intelligent individual who professes to be very passionate about improving the way of life in Delaram. On several occasions Abdul Khaliq has stated that because his tribe is very influential and strong in the area, he has no fear working with the US Marines. While he is suspected of participating in a number of questionable activities, there has been no formal proof of wrongdoing.

The bazaar in Delaram is one of the most prosperous areas in Nimroz due to its position near many major roadways. Vendors line the street selling produce, clothes, and goods from Iran and Pakistan.

PHOTO BY LANCE CPL. BRIAN JONES

Chapter 4
The Economy

The people of Nimroz live at a subsistence level, with an economy based on agriculture, livestock, and the retail trade. The hot desert environment, limited irrigation water, and single growing season make for a poor agricultural economy. Because of the drought of 1997 to 2002, only ten percent of land is cultivated. The principal crops are wheat, maize, melons, watermelons, pomegranates, and poppy. Many inhabitants grow barely enough to feed their own families. Raising livestock was a large business in Nimroz, but the prolonged drought has reduced the industry to less than ten percent of what it used to be. Animal smuggling, of both Afghan animals and those brought in from India, is a source of revenue in the province.

Delaram's thriving bazaar is a rare economic bright spot in the province, with more than 400 small shops that include bakeries, produce stands, mechanical repair garages, dry staples, and beverages. Much of the produce sold in the market comes from Kandahar, Farah City, and Herat, while Nimroz also continues to benefit from trade with Iran. Zaranj, the province's capital, has no industries save for a limited production of handicrafts. A large bazaar is the main boost to the city's struggling economy. An ice factory located in Delaram is one of the only factories in the province. Some domestic crafts and handicrafts are produced for sale in the markets in Nimroz, such as Baluchi carpets and kelims, other

Baluchi handicrafts, spun wool, and animal by-products. Poverty and unemployment drive many people in Zaranj to Iran to seek jobs.

KEY ECONOMIC SECTORS

Agriculture

Agriculture in Nimroz is in dire straits. Areas affected by the drought lack irrigation and fodder for livestock. Since the end of the drought, the lack of water resources and management has devastated the province's agricultural system; only ten percent of land is being cultivated. The irrigation system in Nimroz depends upon rivers and canals, many of which are dry or, in the case of canals, damaged. According to a 2005 UN Office of Drugs and Crime report, when there is enough water to cultivate land, the people of Nimroz grow poppy because its high price will help them recover from prolonged drought.

Pomegranates, grapes, wheat, and maize are the main crops in Khash Rod and Delaram, along with moderate amounts of poppy. Most of the poppy cultivation takes place in Khash Rod district. Before the drought, both districts flourished, cultivating about 20,000 jeribs of land. Since 2002, this has been reduced to only 2,000 jeribs. Many of the districts' major *karezes*—traditional underground canals that irrigate crops— have gone dry and require cleaning. Wealthier farmers have installed tube wells to cultivate their lands, but most cannot afford the expense.

The agriculture sector in Charborjak district was completely destroyed by the drought. Around 85,800 jeribs of land had been previously cultivated in the district; since the drought, there are no known farms in the district. Similarly, Kang district has yet to recover from the drought, and there are no major agricultural activities in the district. Zaranj district has been able to sustain some crops—wheat, maize, melons, watermelons, and some orchard fruit—often only for domestic use.

The majority of land in Nimroz is owned by a few Baluch families known as "Baluch Sardars." Some people own tiny plots of land, but most are tenant farmers. Many landless farmers work as laborers on others' farms in partnership with the landlords, or they lease land from land owners. Laborers are often given shelter and a wage by the landlords. In partnerships (or *bazgari*) between landlords and farmers, landlords give a ratio of the harvest to farmers for cultivating and working the land, similar to sharecropping in the US. In longer-term leases (or *ijara*), farmers lease the land for a fixed number of years for a fixed sum of money or a fixed amount of the harvest.

Livestock

Livestock was once a very important part of people's lives. Oxen, cows, sheep, goats, and camels were all kept in large numbers by many families. But the drought decreased the amount of fodder available for livestock. As a result, livestock numbers have fallen by 90 percent.

The lack of veterinary facilities in the province is also a persistent challenge to families who still own livestock. Some families are involved in the trade of animal and animal products as well as the illegal smuggling of animals to Iran for sale. The most popular animals involved in the illegal trade are oxen and buffalo from India.

Small Business

Delaram has a thriving bazaar of more than 400 shops. Much of the produce sold in the market comes from Kandahar, Farah City, and Herat. Locals have become more confident in the bazaar's future and have begun to invest in its infrastructure by building cement stalls and sidewalks.

Trade

Afghan vehicles are not allowed into Pakistan and Iran, making it difficult to transport fresh food across the borders. Afghan trucks have to change goods from one truck to another at the border, while Pakistani trucks are allowed to cross the border into Afghanistan.

A majority of goods are being imported from Iran, either through legal or illegal channels. Imports include food, construction material, medicines, etc. Animals and animal by-products, such as wool, hide etc., are the main exports to Iran. Nimroz is also a main opium smuggling route between southern Afghanistan and Iran and Pakistan.

POLITICAL ECONOMY

Nimroz produces few commodities that are sold in the regional and global markets, so its agricultural economy is less profitable than those of Kandahar, Farah, and Herat. Because there is not enough water for irrigation and most of the province cannot support industrial farming, the people of Nimroz are occupied primarily in subsistence farming. Although there is a District Rural Rehabilitation and Development (DRRD) office and a District of Agriculture, Irrigation, and Livestock (DAIL) office in Zaranj, representatives of these line ministries are inactive in the districts.

In addition, there are no Afghan agricultural institutions in the province due to a lack of trained agricultural advisors, commonly referred to as extension workers. Important agricultural training in areas of irrigation, alternative crops, fertilizers, and livestock management has been and continues to be neglected. The result is that subsistence level agriculture, with its minimal earning potential, is the only option available for individual farmers.

The Afghanistan International Chamber of Commerce (AICC) and Afghanistan Chamber of Commerce and Industries (ACCI) have offices in Zaranj, but they are hindered by low human resource capacity.

INFRASTRUCTURE

Transportation

Several major paved highways intersect in Delaram in the northeast corner of the province, including Route 1 (Ring Road), which connects it and the province with Kandahar to the east and Farah City and Herat to the west. Roads connecting Zaranj to the districts and the rest of the province are poor, with very few all-weather or asphalt roads.

The intersection of Route 1 with Route 9, and the intersections of Route 1 with Route 512 and 522, makes Delaram a thriving center for trade and services. But insecurity in the neighboring provinces of Helmand and Kandahar, as well as local Taliban activities, often hinders the movement of goods into Delaram.

Zaranj is a key crossing and customs-collection point between Afghanistan and Iran. There is a customs office on the border in Zaranj, and a road connects Zaranj to the Iranian border. Smuggled goods, opium, and manufactured goods such as automobiles, consumer electronics, farming machinery, and clothes pass through Zaranj and up Route 9 to Delaram.

Electricity

According to the 2005 National Risk and Vulnerability Assessment, 38 percent of Nimroz households have electricity, although experienced observers in Delaram believe that estimate is high. Zaranj receives electricity from Iran while other major villages in Nimroz

A small shop in the Delaram bazaar that sells hand-made tools like hatchets. The Delaram bazaar is filled with small shops selling home-made products or goods imported from neighboring Iran or Pakistan. The number of stalls at the bazaar has increased over the past several years due to the improved security situation.

PHOTO BY RICHARD M. CAVAGNOL

rely upon private generators for electricity. USAID has started to introduce solar powered street lights and power for the public health clinic in Delaram.

Irrigation

Irrigation is extremely critical for Nimroz. While much of the province is desert, more than 80 percent of the population depends on farming for their livelihood. The primary sources of flowing water are the Helmand, Khash Rod, and Farah Rivers and their tributaries. Droughts over the past several years have severely impacted the crops, resulting in a subsistence level of farming. Two major canals, Lashkari and Zarkan, were built to facilitate irrigation, but years of war and drought have left them in a state of disrepair. Surveys and international funding suggest that the cleaning and construction of all the traditional canals in all the districts is necessary. The Kamal Khan Dam is still incomplete, but there are plans to construct a dam in Khash Rod district. Karezes exist throughout the province and farmers who can afford it build tube wells.

Drinking Water and Sanitation

On average, only 38 percent of households use safe drinking water. This rises to 45 percent in the rural areas. Although the available figures show that all households in Nimroz have direct access to a main source of drinking water within their community, in many cases this water is contaminated or has a high salt or iron content. On average, only 15 percent of households have access to safe toilet facilities. In urban areas such as Delaram district center, most living compounds simply drill a hole in the compound wall and allow the toilet waste to drain into the street. The few public toilets available in Delaram are in poor repair and have not been cleaned out since 2009.

USAID-sponsored workers prepare a new project in Delaram. USAID currently sponsors two major projects in Nimroz: the Local Governance and Community Development (LGCD) program and the Food Insufficiency Response to Urban Populations (FIRUP) program.

PHOTO BY RICHARD M. CAVAGNOL

Chapter 5
International Organizations and Reconstruction Activities

PROJECTS AND ACTIVITIES

Electricity

About 34 percent of households in Nimroz have electricity.
More than 65 percent of electricity comes from private generators. Small generators and a 20 kW current from Iran power the
capital of Zaranj. There is no electrical grid in Nimroz. USAID is
working with the US Marine Expeditionary Force (MEF) at Camp
Leatherneck in Helmand province to investigate non-fossil fuel
alternative energy sources, such as solar power in Delaram
district, to provide electricity for the bazaar and public health
clinic. The solar power system proposed for the clinic in Delaram
will include a 2.5 kW generator as a backup, along with storage
batteries and an inverter so the relatively few days of rain and
sand storms (which generally last only a few hours in Delaram)
can be handled by the generator. The solar powered street lamps
will not have a generator backup.

Transportation

The major forms of transportation in Nimroz province include bicycles, motor bikes, cars, and buses. The Indian Government's Border Roads Organization built a two-lane paved highway (Route 9) in 2009 from Zaranj through Ghorghori to Delaram. It opened a link between the deep sea port at Chabahar in Iran to Afghanistan's main Ring Road highway system which connects Kabul, Kandahar, Herat, Mazar-e Sharif, and Kunduz. The 215 kilometer-long highway was handed over to Afghan authorities on January 22, 2009.

India plans to build a highway from Zaranj to the free port of Chabahar in Iran, linking the province to the sea. When completed, the road will give Afghanistan a second route to the sea. The current route is through Pakistan to Karachi.

In March 2010 two road projects were completed. A 25 kilometer stretch of road was paved connecting Anar Dara and Pusht Rod districts in Farah with Zaranj. A five kilometer stretch of road in Zaranj was also asphalted. The Anar Dara district road was completed in about a month while the Pusht Rod scheme took nine months to complete.

There was a Pamir Airways air link between Herat and Zaranj, but it was discontinued in early 2010 due to security concerns. Upon taking office, Governor Brahui expressed strong interest in the expansion of the airfield. Due to its proximity to the Iranian border, further refurbishment requires close scrutiny. The US Army Corps of Engineers agreed to expand the current helicopter landing pad.

Irrigation

The Delaram District Support Team (DST) made efforts in 2009 and 2010 to get the Ministry of Rural Reconstruction and Development (MRRD) and Ministry of Agriculture, Irrigation and Livestock (MAIL) to conduct hydrological studies in areas hit hardest by drought and devise a plan for sinking wells for irrigation and drinking water.

In Zaranj district, the USAID FIRUP Irrigation and Drainage program includes lining 28 kilometers of drains with concrete in Zaranj City, clearing 240 kilometers of canals in surrounding villages near Zaranj (including 14 kilometers of the Lashkari Canal and 35 sub-canals located in villages near Zaranj), lining 1,100 meters of existing drains with concrete, constructing 3,550 meters of concrete medians in Zaranj, and planting 6,000 seedlings as part of an erosion prevention effort.

In Chakhansur district, USAID FIRUP program has undertaken the rehabilitation of a major irrigation canal. This project will clear 241.5 kilometers of irrigation canals, construct a six meter retaining wall along Sare Kang main canal, and construct one culvert in Chakhansur. The project is working in coordination with the provincial and district governors, as well as the head of the Provincial Council and the Provincial Irrigation Department.

Additional irrigation work has begun in Khash Rod district with the digging and clearing of 15 kilometers of irrigation canals and drainage ditches in the district center, and the filling and leveling of 5,000 meters of street medians with agricultural soil in the district center.

The Kang irrigation project will specifically dig and clear 36 kilometers of canals, including 11 kilometers of the Sikhsar Canal, the largest canal in Kang District. A small concrete dam will be constructed at the entrance of Sikhsar Canal. Three concrete culverts will also be constructed.

The Khamal Khan Dam project seeks to eliminate flood damage and waterlogging by diverting all flows in excess of beneficial requirements to the Gaud-e Zirreh depression. The project, as envisaged in 1978 by the Ministry of Water and Power, intended to develop about 174,000 hectares of land to a high degree of productivity over a period of 15 to 20 years. Kamal Khan Dam is a controversial project in Iran; it would decrease the supply of water to the already-parched Iranian province of Sistan & Baluchistan to just 26 cubic meters per second. An environmental impact study would be essential for evaluation of the viability of the project.

Little is known of the progress on the Khash Rod Dam.

Sanitation

Workers in Zaranj will construct 100 concrete and brick trash collection points, and remove garbage from all city districts and transport it to the city landfill, where it will be sorted and then burned or buried as appropriate. This project was initiated in response to requests from the provincial governor and mayor of Zaranj. In Khash Rod local workers are building 20 garbage collection sites, and a program of daily garbage collection has been instituted.

Education

The overall literacy rate in Nimroz is 22 percent, in part because the mainly rural population of about 100,000 people is spread across 41,356 sq km of the province. Nearly one third of men are literate (30 percent) compared to only about one tenth of women (11 percent). Among people between 15 and 24 years of age, 44 percent of men and only ten percent of women are literate. The Kuchi population in the province has particularly low levels of literacy—less than one percent of men and no women are able to read or write.

On average 33 percent of children between 6 and 13 are enrolled in school. The figure is better for boys with nearly three out of five enrolled (39 percent) than for girls with just over a quarter (26 percent) enrolled. Among the Kuchi population, there are no children attending school.

There are 62 primary and secondary schools in the province catering to 33,926 students. Boys account for 63 percent of students and 89 percent of schools are boys' schools. There are 721 teachers working in Nimroz, with varying levels of training and preparation. Among teachers, 39 percent are women.

A number of Afghans cross the border into Iran for technical and skills training. Iran has set up some small technical and vocational training schools in Nimroz to train youth for construction and manufacturing trades.

Healthcare

Much of the population of Nimroz does not have access to health care, but a basic infrastructure of health services is available in provincial population centers. There are 15 basic health centers (BHC), one comprehensive health center (CHC), and one hospital with a total of 30 beds.

The BHC is a small facility that offers limited curative care, including diagnosis and treatment of malaria, diarrhea, and acute respiratory infection; distribution of condoms and oral contraceptives, and subsequent depot progesterone (DMPA) injections; and micronutrient supplementation. The BHC health care workers are responsible for treating illnesses and conditions common in children and adults. Female health workers, such as midwives, focus on providing care for normal deliveries, identifying danger signs, and referring potentially problematic pregnancies to the CHC.

An intensive care unit nurse provides medical assistance to two Afghan civilians. Only about 22 doctors and 64 nurses are active in the province as of 2009. They serve less than three percent of the population.

PHOTO BY CPL. MATTHEW TROYER

Services offered include antenatal, delivery, and postpartum care, nonpermanent family planning, routine immunizations, integrated management of childhood diseases, treatment of malaria and tuberculosis, and identification, referral, and follow-up care for mental patients and the disabled.

The services of the BHC cover a population of 15,000 to 30,000, depending on the local geographic conditions and the population density. In circumstances where the population is very isolated, the minimum population for a BHC can be less than 15,000. The minimal staffing requirements for a BHC are a nurse, a community midwife, and two vaccinators.

The CHC covers a larger area of 30,000 to 60,000 people and offers a wider range of services than the BHC. In addition to assisting normal deliveries, the CHC can handle some complications, grave cases of childhood illness, treatment of complicated cases of malaria, and outpatient care for mental patients and the disabled. The facility has limited space for inpatient care, but has a laboratory. The staff of a CHC is also larger than that of a BHC; it includes both male and female doctors, male and female nurses, midwives, and laboratory and pharmacy technicians.

In 2009 there were about 22 doctors and 64 nurses employed by the Ministry of Health working in the province. Less than three percent of the population is able to take advantage of these existing health facilities, and of those, almost 68 percent must travel more than ten kilometers.

Security

The UN Office on Drugs and Crime will construct a regional border security garrison—a large regional center that can support 100 to 200 troops—which will help Afghan Border Police and other counter narcotics agencies work together in the region. This enhanced base of operations will be strategically placed in the tactical crossroads of the Nimroz smuggling routes, and will put adequate numbers of properly trained and equipped police officers in proper position to interdict large numbers of international smugglers who currently move freely through this area.

DISTRICT SUPPORT TEAM (DST)

The USG civilian presence in Nimroz consists of a District Support Team, with a USAID Field Program Officer and a Department of State Representative located in Delaram. While there is no PRT in Nimroz province, the DST maintains close coordination, communication, and cooperation with the Farah and Helmand PRTs and with the Marine Expeditionary Headquarters and the G-9 at Camp Leatherneck. The DST works with the Marine Civil Affairs Group (CAG) on economic development projects identified and prioritized by the Delaram community council (as of 2010, there is no Community Development Council (CDC) in Delaram) and the Delaram district governor. There are two major USAID projects—the Local Governance and Community Development (LGCD) program implemented by USAID's partner, Development Alternatives Incorporated (DAI); and the Food Insufficiency Response to Urban Populations (FIRUP) program implemented by USAID's partner, the Central Asia Development Group (CADG). Both programs focus on community-based projects at the local government level.

These projects are implemented in conjunction with the US Department of Defense Commander's Emergency Response Program (CERP) funds, administered by the Marine CAG. The projects under these programs are typically labor-intensive and are aimed at getting the unemployed segments of the population to work. Zaranj and Delaram are the main focus of these activities, with some projects beginning in Khash Rod during the fall of 2010. Each project is dependent upon the local security situation. The ultimate goal is to develop sustainable businesses and government services that will continue after the USAID and CERP funding has ended.

In late 2010 President Karzai announced that private security firms would be banned from working in Afghanistan. This ban, which goes into effect in February 2011, would forbid development firms and non-governmental organizations from employing private security guards to protect their personnel or projects. An estimated $1.4 billion of development projects risk being shut down.

NATIONAL SOLIDARITY PROGRAM

The National Solidarity program (NSP) is a nation-wide, grass-roots development program administered through the Ministry of Rural Rehabilitation and Development (MRRD) which focuses on the 80 percent of the population that live in rural areas of the country. MRRD is responsible for determining what constitutes a community (50 or more families), the size of the block grant, and the geographic areas targeted for the grants. The MRRD is also in charge of the overall execution of the program, including fund raising, communication, program monitoring, and contracting the external evaluators.

Through the administration of block grants, managed by the elected members of the Community Development Council (CDC), this program places rural development in the hands of the local population. Several of the Nimroz districts are reported to have CDCs who prioritize, plan, and implement local development projects such as irrigation systems and road construction that benefit the whole community. However, little is known of these councils and their activities. As of 2010, no known NGOs or UN organizations were working in Nimroz province.

Local Afghans enjoy tea in the marketplace. Word of mouth is the primary way in which people learn about events and exchange ideas. Men will often gather around to drink tea and exchange ideas and stories.

PHOTO BY LANCE CPL. BRIAN JONES

Chapter 6
Information and Influence

INFORMATION SHARING AND NETWORKS

Roughly 80 percent of the Nimroz population lives in rural villages that range from 25 to 500 families. Without a provincial electrical grid, the use of radio and television media is generally confined to the urban area of Zaranj. The lack of electricity, low average annual wage, and high illiteracy make word of mouth the most common method of spreading news and information in Nimroz province. Information, gossip, and news are shared at many informal gatherings at restaurants and small tea shops in the bazaar. The few people who have access to a radio or satellite TV share what they hear with their fellow villagers.

In Delaram, the district governor entertains a steady stream of groups of local men to discuss business and catch up on local news. Often the DST is invited to the district governor's house for tea to listen to what is happening in the district center and the outlying rural villages. The mullahs also play a key role in sharing information and influencing the population, especially in rural areas. Prayer time at the mosques, especially Friday prayer in community mosques, brings people together to gossip and share information.

The Pashtun and Baluchs of Nimroz are generally suspicious of strangers, especially foreigners. Even in large communities such as Delaram with 8,000 or more inhabitants, a stranger will be immediately identified either by dress, accent, or habits. This makes it difficult to obtain information about the individual, community, or culture. Information about the community can only be obtained once rapport and trust are established with the locals. The Human Terrain Team (HTT), which lives and works closely with the DST, was able to conduct interviews of a number of key leaders in Delaram. This information substantially contributed to the development of an overall picture of what was happening in Delaram and surrounding villages.

The Taliban and other insurgents circulate "night letters" in mosques and villages, targeting individuals and even whole organizations for death if they cooperate with ISAF and US forces. The Taliban also use hand-held radios to discuss plans and coordinate activities.

TELECOMMUNICATIONS

A recent expansion in the number of cell phone towers in Nimroz has made coverage significantly better in every district. The two major cell phone carriers are Roshan Wireless and Afghan Wireless Communication Company (AWCC). AWCC is the most widely used service in Nimroz. The wide use of cellular phones has sped up the information sharing networks for both good and ill. The Taliban use the cellular network to track the movement of ISAF troops and to plan activities. Civilians use it to share information about politics and corruption in the government, to look for education opportunities, and to job hunt. In Delaram, AWCC has a standing arrangement with the Taliban to shut down from 6:00 pm to 6:00 am. The Taliban do not want citizens reporting their movement at night and have agreed not to destroy AWCC towers as long as the blackout continues.

MEDIA

There is no radio station in Delaram, and the number of radio stations in Zaranj and other district centers is unknown. The principal means of sharing information is by cell phone and through face-to-face meetings and public gatherings in the bazaar and mosques.

Television

Television stations do not exist in Delaram because there is no public electricity grid. Most of the population cannot afford a television set anyway. The number of television stations in Zaranj is unknown, although there have been reports of Nimroz public and cable television stations in operation. People who do have satellite systems power them with private or local village generators, and receive their programs from India, Pakistan, and Iran.

Radio

The number and type of radio stations in Zaranj and in the other district capitals is unknown. There is no radio station in Delaram because there is no public electricity grid. The US Marines, in conjunction with the DST, use Radio in a Box (RIAB) to broadcast messages to the population who have received solar- and battery-powered radios from USAID and the Marine Civil Affairs Group (CAG). The Marine Information Operations team collects and disseminates messages from the district governor, USAID agricultural messages, and local news and weather.

Print

The number and names of the newspapers in Nimroz province is unknown. In Delaram district, the area under control of ISAF, there were no newspapers in 2010 due to the illiteracy rate. Billboards along Route 1 are predominantly graphic with little or no text.

An officer gives each soldier his salary in Zaranj. Corruption runs rampant throughout the province. For example, many police officers will take a commission from soldiers' pay. Police are also accused of taking money from people at checkpoints along the highway.

PHOTO BY ROMESH BHATTACHARJI

Chapter 7
The Big Issues

SECURITY

The population of Nimroz sees security as the major issue requiring improvement. In Delaram, the only area with ISAF presence, there are a relatively small number of local Taliban, estimated to be between 15 and 25. Nevertheless, through intimidation and threats—including the assassination of the mayor in January 2009—they have been able to instill fear in the population, which has become reluctant to talk with ISAF and DST personnel or accept work on USAID projects. This is especially true in the rural villages, such as the 21 villages located to the northeast and southwest of Delaram along the Khash Rod River. Villages such as Dehmazang, which are 30 kilometers from the Delaram district center, feel isolated, and the ANP outposts are attacked and harassed by the Taliban on a regular basis.

The Delaram district governor believes that the large numbers of IEDs planted in Delaram are brought in by Taliban from Bakwa district in Farah to the west or Washer district in Helmand to the east. The district governor has continually requested additional ANP from Zaranj to beef up the current force of 45 officers, but the presence of the large Marine Forward Operating Base (FOB) and the 215th Afghan National Army Corps headquarters in Delaram has prevented him from receiving additional resources. The addition of a Georgian battalion has increased the security at the ANP station and around the bazaar, but a number of the local residents see the Georgians as Russians, which triggers bad memories of the Soviet occupation.

POROUS BORDERS

Afghanistan's borders with Iran and Pakistan are highly porous and poorly patrolled. Many Afghans cross the border illegally for work. Opiates, precursor chemicals, weapons, ammunition, IED components, and foreign military advisors for the Taliban cross these borders easily. In July 2009 the provincial governor announced that Afghan security forces in the province had arrested seven would-be suicide bombers, including three Iranian nationals carrying suicide vests. In October 2010 the chief police officer in Nimroz announced that the ANP had discovered 19 tons of explosives in an Iranian shipment of food and aid.

Poppy is grown in relatively small quantities in Nimroz compared to Helmand and other provinces, but the large, unpatrolled border has made Nimroz the main gateway for smuggling opium, morphine, and heroin out of Afghanistan. The intersection of Route 1 (Ring Road), Route 9, Route 522, and Route 512 in Delaram, as well as the crossing points into and out of Iran at Zaranj makes it easy to move goods quickly between Herat, Farah City, Delaram, Gulistan, Zaranj, and Iran.

The ANP checkpoints do not stop smuggling because a significant number of ANP officers receive bribes and payoffs from drug traffickers. In addition, the number of local border police has diminished in the region due to lack of support, equipment, training, and facilities. Law enforcement agencies in both countries are institutionally weak, short of resources, or otherwise unable to stop the movement of illegal goods, from weapons to drugs.

Iran would certainly like to stop the drug trade to and from Afghanistan. The UN Office on Drugs and Crime (UNODC) estimates that Iran has up to 1.7 million opiate addicts, making it a major hub for the drug trade. This provides a highly lucrative market for drugs transiting through Nimroz.

RELATIONS WITH IRAN AND PAKISTAN

Iran has provided aid for infrastructure and reconstruction efforts in Nimroz. It has also allowed Afghans to attend schools in Iran that provide vocational and technical training, and it has built and staffed several training facilities in Nimroz. The Zaranj branch of Iran's Imam Khomeini Relief Committee, the organization's third largest office in Afghanistan, claimed to have assisted 7,500 Nimroz residents between March 2008 and March 2009. The Imam Khomeini Relief Committee is not solely a charity agency; both inside and outside Iran, it works closely with the Islamic Revolutionary Guard Corps.

Water rights to the Helmand River remain an issue of contention between Iran and Afghanistan. The Afghan government began building the Kamal Khan Dam in the 1970s, but the Soviet invasion left the project incomplete. To this day, Iran opposes the project's completion because it relies on the water from the Helmand River to irrigate its agriculture.

Disputes over the rate and manner of Iran's repatriation of Afghan refugees are a constant irritant in Afghanistan's relationship with Iran. In November and December 2008 Afghan authorities accused Iran of dumping 1,000 Afghan refugees a day in Nimroz without coordination. In May 2010 Amrullah Sultani, the top Afghan official responsible for refugees in Nimroz accused the Iranian government of expelling over 60,000 Afghan refugees to the province over two months without prior coordination with the provincial officials.

Nimroz has an extensive border with Pakistan's Baluchistan province. Ethnic Baluchs live on both sides of the Afghan-Baluchistan border as well as in neighboring Iran. It took seven months after the partition of India and the creation of Pakistan for the Pakistani government to quash Baluchi pretensions of independence under the Khan of Kalat. Pakistani authorities have faced an on-again, off-again Baluch insurgency ever since. In order to counter this ethno-national sentiment, some inside Pakistan helped empower Islamist movements in the area. While Pakistan no longer overtly supports the Taliban, insurgents have used Baluchistan and its capital, Quetta, as a sanctuary and base of operations throughout Operation Enduring Freedom.

In addition, Afghanistan and Pakistan are trying to resolve issues such as border security, immigration, smuggling, and trade. Iran, Pakistan, and Afghanistan hold regular meetings at the head of state and ministerial levels regarding issues that affect the "golden triangle" where Iran, Baluchistan, and Afghanistan intersect.

GOVERNMENT LEGITIMACY

The degree of success of a government is directly related to the level of perceived legitimacy of the government and its officials. The current Afghan government is highly centralized, with most fiscal and political power located in the country's capital. Unfortunately, this style of government has failed to incorporate the dynastic tribal elders and religious tribal mullahs. Many rural Afghans identify more with their village and their qawm than the province or country as a whole. The Taliban, who are a complex network of insurgent groups with various tribal loyalties, have been able to exploit locals' fear of an imposing centralized authority.

High level and widespread corruption and elections fraud, coupled with poorly trained inexperienced government officials, further challenge the legitimacy of the government and contribute to the dissatisfaction of the population with the central government. ISAF has begun to focus more on re-empowering the village elders and mullahs through Community Development Councils (CDCs) and other local governance schemes. Some believe that the reestablishment of local legitimacy will deny the Taliban political control.

Naan is a staple at most Afghan meals, especially breakfast. It is normally paired with tea and possibly milk or butter. After breakfast, men traditionally go to work at a farm or bazaar while women remain at the family compound.

PHOTO BY 1ST LT. CHRISTINE A. DARIUS

APPENDICES

TIMELINE OF KEY EVENTS

June 2002: Abdul Karim Brahui appointed governor of Nimroz province by President Hamid Karzai.

June 2005: Dr. Ghulam Dastagir Azad replaces Abdul Karim Brahui as governor of Nimroz.

October 2008: US Marines build a Forward Operating Base in Delaram and begin to patrol the district.

October 2009: The first US government civilian presence in Nimroz, a District Support Team (DST), sets up at the Afghan National Police (ANP) station in Delaram. The DST consists of one USAID Field Program Officer and one Department of State Foreign Service Officer.

November 2009: Asadullah Haqdost named district governor of Delaram.

December 2009: USAID begins implementation of economic development projects under the Local Governance and Community Development (LGCD) and Food Insufficiency Response to Urban Populations (FIRUP) programs.

January 2010: Delaram mayor Abdullah Jan assassinated in the Delaram bazaar. He is replaced by Noor Alah.

May 2010: Nine suicide bombers disguised as police storm the provincial council office in Zaranj, killing a woman council member, two policemen, and a visitor. All the attackers die. Provincial Council moves to Kabul as a result.

August 2010: Abdul Karim Brahui replaces Dr. Ghulam Dastagir Azad as governor of Nimroz.

COMMON COMPLIMENTS REGARDING ISAF IN NIMROZ

- Afghans respect the ISAF troops for leaving their families to come to Afghanistan to help them.

- Afghans compliment the ISAF troops on their work ethic which often inspires the Afghans to work harder.

- Afghans welcome development projects that improve the infrastructure of the province and put people to work.

- Where other foreign armies have come to Afghanistan to conquer the people, ISAF has come to help the people.

COMMON COMPLAINTS REGARDING ISAF IN NIMROZ

- Afghans claim that when ISAF troops are attacked by insurgents, ISAF sometimes retaliates against innocent people.

- Afghans complain that when ISAF troops go into the bazaar with their armored vehicles, it drives away business from their shops.

- Afghans complain that ISAF troops drive down the middle of the road and force Afghan vehicles off the road.

- Afghans complain that ISAF troops raid their houses at night without cause or Afghan government support.

- Afghans complain that ISAF troops support the Afghan National Police (ANP) who are corrupt.

A DAY IN THE LIFE OF A RURAL NIMROZI

Rural Nimrozi live in mud, straw, and wood houses which may or may not be surrounded by a wall. They begin their days with the imam's call to prayer one hour before sunrise. Men get up and wash in accordance with Islamic tradition before going to their village mosque for the first of five prayers of the day. Women pray at home, start a fire, and prepare breakfast. While breakfast is being prepared, young boys and girls receive religious instruction at the local mosque after the prayer. They return for a breakfast that consists of *naan* bread and green tea, a staple in most houses of Nimroz. This might be supplemented with milk and butter for those who have cattle. Sugar is usually served only to guests.

After breakfast, the men go to the fields or, if they work in a bazaar such as Delaram, they will walk or take a motor bike to their stall. Families prepare children for school if one is available; schools are more likely in cities and towns than in the countryside. In rural areas, school may be held in a private home or in the village mosque, where the village mullah serves as the teacher. Boys are far more likely to attend school than girls. If they are not in school, young boys and girls who have not reached physical maturity help to graze the cattle or sheep. The older boys help their fathers in the field. Children also help with the wheat and poppy harvests. Migrant laborers are often hired to harvest poppy, which is very labor intensive. Insurgent activity tends to drop off for about two weeks during this harvest period, usually in April or May. Women do not work outside the home and do not leave the family compound unless it is to visit relatives or attend weddings or festivals. Sometimes on Fridays, women meet to sing or recite the Koran.

Usually everyone returns home for lunch at midday, but sometimes men will stay in the field. A typical lunch for a Nimrozi is rice with cooked vegetables, and is often accompanied by yogurt and slices of onion or other fresh vegetables such as tomatoes and okra from the fields. Meat will usually be served at the evening meal if it is available. If a family kills a sheep or a goat, it will usually share the meat with its neighbors because the meat will spoil quickly in the hot seasons. Families will store pomegranates, almonds, and raisins to supplement their diet during the winter months. In the evening, light is provided by propane or kerosene lamps.

FURTHER READING AND SOURCES

Books

- *ISAF PRT Handbook*, 4th Ed. NATO, June 2009.

- Louis Dupree, *Afghanistan,* Princeton: Princeton University Press, 1979.

- Stephen Tanner, *Afghanistan: A Military History from Alexander the Great to the War Against the Taliban*, Philadelphia: Da Capo Press, 2009.

- Robert D. Crews and Amin Trazi (eds), *The Taliban and the Crisis of Afghanistan*, Boston: Harvard University Press, 2008.

- Edward Girardet and Jonathan Walter, *Afghanistan: Essential Field Guides to the Humanitarian and Conflict Zone*, Crosslines Publication Ltd., 1998 and 2004, *www.crosslinesguides.com*.

- Ahmed Rashid, *Descent into Chaos: The United States and the Future of Nation Building in Afghanistan, Pakistan, and Central Asia*, New York: Viking Press, 2008.

- Ahmed Rashid, *Taliban: Militant Islam, Oil and Fundamentalism in Central Asia*, New Haven: Yale University Press, 2010.

- Larry Goodson, *Afghanistan's Endless War: State Failure, Regional Politics, and the Rise of the Taliban*, Olympia: University of Washington Press, 2001.

- Greg Mortenson, *Three Cups of Tea: One Man's Mission to Promote Peace...One School at a Time*, New York: Penguin Books, 2007.

- Barnett Rubin, *The Fragmentation of Afghanistan*, New Haven: Yale University Press, 2002.

- Barnett Rubin, *Afghanistan's Uncertain Transition from Turmoil to Normalcy*, Washington, D.C.: Council on Foreign Relations, 2007.

- Michael Griffin, *Reaping the Whirlwind: The Taliban Movement in Afghanistan*, London: Pluto Press, 2001.

- Steve Coll, *Ghost Wars: The Secret History of the CIA, Afghanistan, and Bin Laden, From the Soviet Invasion to September 10, 2001*, New York: Penguin Press, 2004.

- Marc Sageman, *Understanding Terrorist Networks*, Philadelphia: University of Pennsylvania Press, 2004.

- Patrick Clawson and Michael Rubin, Eternal Iran: Continuity and Chaos, New York: Palgrave, 2005.

Articles and Documents

- *"Afghanistan,"* 2007 CIA World Factbook, *https://www.cia.gov/library/publications/the-world-factbook/* (June 8, 2007).

- *"Provincial Profile,"* Nimroz, Ministry of Rural Rehabilitation and Development and the National Area Base Development Programme, 2006, *www.mrrd.gov.af/* (February 29, 2008).

- *"Provincial Overview—Nimroz Province,"* Monterey: Program for Cultural and Conflict Studiers, Naval Postgraduate School, 2008, *www.nps.edu/programs/ccs/Docs/ExecutiveSummaries/Nimroz_Prov_Overview_CCS.pdf.*

- Regional Rural Economic Development Strategies (RREDS), *Provincial Profile for Nimroz*, 2006, *http://www.aisa.org.af/english/brochures.*

- The Afghanistan National Development Strategy (ANDS) 2008-2013, Hamid Karzai, *www.embassyofafghanistan.org/documents/resume_ANDS.pdf.*

- National Risk and Vulnerability Survey 2007-8, Central Statistics Office. *http://nrva.cso.gov.af/NRVA2007-08Report.pdf.*

- Sub-National Governance policy *(approved by Afghan Cabinet on March 22).*

- *"Report on Progress Toward Security and Stabilization in Afghanistan,"* DoD, (April 2010).

- *"United States Government Integrated Civilian-Military Campaign Plan for Support to Afghanistan," www.comw.org/qdr/fulltext/ 0908eikenberryandmcchrystal.pdf* (August 10, 2010).

- Afghanistan and Pakistan Regional Stabilization Strategy (January 10, 2010).

- "Baluchistan," *Oxford Encyclopedia of the Modern World,* New York: Oxford University Press, 2008.

Websites

- Afghanistan Research and Evaluation Unit, *The A to Z Guide to Afghanistan Assistance 2010, www.reliefweb.int/rw/RWFiles2010. nsf/FilesByRWDocUnidFilename/ASAZ-84PCAT-full_report. pdf/$File/full_report.pdf*

- Afghanistan Information Management Services, *www.aims.org.af*

- USAID, *www.usaid.gov/locations/asia/countries/afghanistan*

- Naval Postgraduate School Program for Cultural and Conflict Studies, *www.nps.edu/Programs/CCS/index.html*

- "The Afghan Analyst," *http://afghanistan-analyst.org*

- Afghanistan Research and Evaluation Unit (AREU), *www.areu.org.af*

- Harmonie Web, *https://ronna-afghan.harmonieweb.org/Pages/ Default.aspx*

www.ingramcontent.com/pod-product-compliance
Lightning Source LLC
Chambersburg PA
CBHW040127270326
41927CB00001B/21